YENDOR D. WOLF

HAIKU WRITER AND MARTIAL ARTIST EXTRAORDINAIRE

Presents

THE WOLF'S TRAVELS

VOLUME 1: THE CITY

The Wolf's Travels by Yendor D. Wolf

Copyright © 2016

All rights reserved. This book or any portion thereof may not be produced or used in any manner whatsoever without the express written permission of the publisher except for the use of brief quotations in a book review.

Printed in the United States of America

First Printing, 2016

ISBN 978-1-945777-03-5

Dedication

This book is dedicated to Master Jack and all people who face their battles head-on.

"The power of your strike comes from absolute conviction and proper character. Understand yourself thoroughly so you may never throw a weak punch."

Master Jack

Introduction

Congratulations, you are reading the first of a three volume series of haikus.

This is the first official book from Yendor D. Wolf, Martial Artist and Haiku Writer Extraordinaire. Since his tenure at 5/7/5 Magazine, he traveled the nation recording his encounters, thoughts, and feelings in haiku form. During this time, he also defended his position as the World's Strongest Fighter in the World Adult Fighting League (WAFL).

This first volume spans the beginning of his journey: Leaving his home and Master to embrace the world and hone his martial and artistic crafts in the City.

Message from Yendor D. Wolf:

Thank you for reading my book. This is not only a solid work, but evidence that dreams can be fulfilled with discipline and patience.

I'll describe the types of haikus featured in the 3 volumes:

The 1st volume shows haiku in the 5-7-5 syllable format. I like playing with this style. It's like trying to fit a world into a box; you make the most of limited space.

The 2nd volume focuses on brevity in haiku.

The 3rd volume utilizes different writing techniques (e.g. Narrowing Focus, Sense Switching, & Riddle Technique) and features more Senryu.

The pocket watch glows
Under the pale, moonlit sky
With evanescence[i]

The enchanted dance
Then a hearty, tasty brunch
Fills my appetite[ii]

That harsh winter storm
Comes to devour us all
Bring your hot cocoa[iii]

All these life troubles
At most exuberant fears
Of failing strange quests

Place life in a cup…
Drink up its voracious juice
Heave the crappy pits

It's my own design!
This world you run freely in.
Created from death...

Take a left on Hell,
Then turn back on Heaven's gates,
Meet me at Earth's edge[IV]

Fortune Cookie Crisp
Receive counsel from a box
Of Confucian Joy

Will love come to me
With a delicious fervor
Or walk idly by[v]

Grab your shoes and ride
On this funky odyssey
Such superb style[vi]

What's a Space Cowboy?
A splendiferous hunter
Delivering cool

Your mind's small Eden
Contains small lavish treasures
Shimmering with bliss[vii]

Small sandy pebbles
Support my brown feet and toes
A lift in spirits[viii]

The changing seasons
Pass by with hazy brilliance
Masked in snowy sun

A samurai's mind
Cuts through with contemplation
To strike ignorance

When did you decide
To pluck the fickle tight strings
Of this wayward life

I don't understand
This elusive view called Hope
Under the cold rain

Thirty days of grief
Ten months of cankerous angst
Shifts to jolly bliss

Wine and dine at 8
With candle-lit stars gleaming
Upon your soft face

These old hazel eyes
See the dynamite neon
In your expression[ix]

Once you are up there
Look down on the golden fields
Witness misfortune

Twenty days of rain
Flash flood in February
I have yet to wake

What is there to do?
There's been a lot of drinking
Up here in Heaven[x]

When lost in romance
Spare neither Self nor a dime
Else you a sucka

Escape to the dark
Vanish into the bleakness
To see what you missed

A girl with flowers
A brazenly, humdrum man
To be continued…

Wake up this monster
With your fabulous fanfare
Of the bodacious

On the Spring retreat
He receives an apple pie
Freshly baked and square

The blue hummingbird
Hums to and fro from its perch
Landing on the air

White haberdashers
Vacate the inner street maze
Away from Wal-Mart

Face the new midnight
With a turn of consciousness
Straight to the aware

Differentiate.
Apply your algorithm
To solve for today

And with so few words
You break your beloved's heart
Destroyer of worlds[xi]

Take it back, erase
All melancholy and fear
Just to grin again

Kites are for great fun
Not for simple enjoyment
Complexly carefree

Too cuckoo emu
Chews all that fat with the Cat
It must be April

We all have mistakes
Tucked away in our pockets
Just for safe keeping[xii]

There goes the haughty
Jive turkeys selling their wares
Makes all us plain fools

Behold! The Great Sun!
Purveyor of life and heat
Shine! Baby mine soul!

Witness the Pale Moon!
Invigorates the Cool Night
With Grace and Guile

OH? Those nimble children?
The ones who'll paint the future?
Let them paint themselves

No worries Old Man
The day has yet to slumber
We can still fly kites

Now, without a doubt
The baby can live without
A pacifier

The Wolf lives Alone
The Wolf resides in a Pack
The Wolf is Center[xiii]

No worries for this
Complex exchange between us
I'll go through my phone

Clumsy Teenager
Smugly wears his mauve medal
With the war-torn men

Shriveled, Mad Old Man
Grumbles at the feisty kids
You had a chance too

I'll get what I want
This time and all other times
Emotions be damned

A Chaste hummingbird
Wallows and sighs in the reeds
Falling, bit by bit

I will remember
Your dance, smile, and spirit
Lying frozen here[xiv]

Look at the Robot
Eating, projecting, learning
Such a cute being

I guess we'll have sex
Like pants hating wolverines
We'll rip and snarl

Touch me, feel me, Hon
Hold me, Squeeze me, Love me, Babe
Only when I want

Find your inner Spark,
In the heat of the night, Son
That's where your Truth lies

Under the snow-rain
Only outside the city
Does the Lone Wolf cry

Only in your eyes
The Night begins to Shine Bright
Sweetening this tale

Come on, boogie down
Make up that mind of yours, Jack
Shine your Will on us

Dragons fly above
Nuzzles against brittle clouds
Scratches itchy backs[xv]

The deserted road...
Not enough room for my doubts
Only solitude

There's less of this book
Than what you have read so far
Put yourself in this[xvi]

Let's make a drawing
Place a circle around here
Now, draw with whimsy

Dirt and Grime cover
The remains of our success
Clean it with passion

The Street Samurai
Do not approach for risk of
Offending his pride

Dust clouds rolled inside
This humble and small homestead,
Covering our goods[xvii]

I read the story
Page by page within your eyes
What language is this

I can't go to school
I'm training for the real world
I'm not good at rote

When we are dancing
Illuminating the place
Don't let go of me

Parking the car here
I stared at the hospital
Then I fled inward

A note arrived here
The Devil delivered it
Such sweet penmanship

There is coziness
It coddles with a blanket
Unlike contentment

First, there is the meat
Let's tenderize and season
Next step, just cook it

I will never paint
I will never write or dance
But I will enjoy

The Great Space Dandy
Finds Action among the Stars
But not his bedroom

Pride and Prejudice
Skipping along the star path
Homogeneous

'No understanding'
There is no worse fate for us
Than no listening

I've sold emotions...
The highest bidders were all
Tough and stoic men

Step up to the Court!
Godzilla Getting' Busy!
Take it to the Hole!

This, the last Donut
A final refuge from life
Full from emptiness

Godzilla Got Friends
Godzilla finds his true love
Goodbye Godzilla[xviii]

Create your gift well
Perfect necessary skills
So that it may shine

We all wish to rule
We all want control of things
Mostly ourselves

"Master, how are you?"
"Sad Yendor, but still happy.
You're off to explore."[XIX]

"It won't be for long."
"I know Yendor, but I don't.
That is what scares me."

"I will do my best."
"You will, but life is fussy.
It can trip you up."

"I'll watch out for it."
"I believe you, I'll relax.
Life also provides."

"What should I accept?"
"I'm still choosing for myself.
It's not up to me."

"How can I decide?"
"Pressure from the shifting winds,
The beat of your heart."

"But they're not in sync."
"Give more time for reflection.
They will balance out."

"I am going now."
"I'm surprised you stayed so long.
Thank you for the time."

"I love you, Master."
"I love you too, my Student.
Go make yourself proud."

The Master sat there
Every muscle motionless
Wind comforting him

The Student steps out
No grand gesture, not one doubt
Into the city

Patience endures all...
Combat, a requirement...
Loving...that's tough work

A beguiling task,
Self-Actualization,
Requires hard work

An empty rice sack
Is ultimately useless
Holding back a door

In order to kill
Prove the other as crazy
Hate will take over

To provide shelter
See the other as yourself
Peace will take over

Let your mind wander
Let your mind unfix itself
Be still, no movement

"On being simple..."
An arduous task for man
Such an endeavor!

The Hummingbird sits
But cannot stay for too long
Legs weren't meant to stand

Haibun

Already a few months in the City and I'm still looking for a place to sleep, a new home to develop techniques, and a healthy living. I'm a vagabond using the café tables as a rest stop before more apartment hunting or until a waiter tells me to leave. Without Master's guidance, the path looks murkier and feels out of line with my goal.

I feel guilty, sometimes, for not taking advantage of being the 'World's Strongest'. It's hard to when my other passion is unrecognized, seen as only a hobby by most, unsustainable by the rest. But to fight for money? The Wolf Style is my chosen way of life. Making it a living feels odd.

With the day split between training and writing, fretting about living, and quiet malaise, it's hard to step back and consider if I made the right choice. Master had a saying for these occasions, 'You never know if you made the right choice until you get far enough down the road. By then, you already decided.'

I'll give this more time.

Old Duck, Young Duck swim
    Wading in the River Grand
        The youngling flies off…

i This book contains endnotes explaining the author's mindset and environment on selected haikus.

ii This is his first one night stand in the city. He met a girl impressed with fighting, but nothing more.

iii Winter arrives with a heavy helping of snow. Not an unusual sight for him but this is the first time he didn't shovel snow in the village where he used to live. Instead there's a bonding moment with his cantankerous roommate, Cat.

iv This is his training regimen and how he approaches writing as well.

v A simple question with varying answers.

vi It was the Funk Friday Faraday Festival. His fighting partner, Kelly, convinces him to breaking out of his shell.

vii A conversation with another martial artist helps him gain perspective and hope for his journey.

viii At the beach, he reminisces about his Master and their beach days. He watches the small crabs and seashells move with the tide.

ix Master Jack always had an appreciation for enthusiastic beginners in the martial arts. He expresses this sentiment the best way he can.

x He reflects on the various religions and their aspects of the afterlife. The prospect of eternal bliss never appealed to him.

xi He knew the relationship wouldn't last but he still did not prepare for the fallout.

xii He expresses how people move about life with new experiences.

xiii He describes his fighting style, Wolf Style (Kombat de Lou).

xiv He finds someone crying on the sidewalk next to a bloody body. After calling the authorities he stays with that person, comforting him as best as he could.

xv He sits at the park and watches the annual kite festival. He saw a dragon kite breeze by clouds.

xvi He wants the reader to write in the margins and interpret each haiku separately from the endnotes. He believes haikus can have dual meanings, one for the individual and one for the writer.

xvii While arguing with his roommate, he senses the issue wasn't about them or the unwashed dishes. He asks if the quarrel was about anything else. She yells and went to her room.

xviii This haiku, similar to the one on pg. 77, is a reference, and small tribute to, a future Beats Master named Groovy Godzilla.

xix The following haikus (pgs. 81–92) are a dream conversation he had with his Master the night before leaving for the city, 7 days after Master Jack's death.

www.ingramcontent.com/pod-product-compliance
Lightning Source LLC
Chambersburg PA
CBHW021155080526
44588CB00008B/354